BEST WAY TO BECOME SUCCESSFUL
Small Business Management

By

Francois Demezier

Copyrights

DEDICATION

I dedicate that book to my wife, Rose Catia Demezier, which allowed me to finalize this book, which requests various sacrifices. Thank you for believe in me and make sure I have a great environment to concretize my dreams. You are the most caring, smart, beautiful, loving, and fantastic woman I knew for my entire life.

Also, I want to dedicate my book to my two little girls - Francesca M Demezier, six years old, and Fanechka Demezier, three years old - for being the most enjoyable thing in my life. Thank you for helping me sometimes disconnect to my writing, and playing with me, making me laugh, and create a new path for my taught.

A special dedication to my brother Barthelemy J. Demezier, for his, advises his support, and his ideas. Without your invitation, I would not be in the Life Insurance field, opening my mind broadly. I am grateful for having you as an elder brother.

I dedicate my book to these two people; my father, Cabeche Demezier, and my mother, Merita Floreal. I will never be who I am if you did not make all the sacrifices for me. I will never thank you enough.

PREFACE

Life makes of passion, project, dreams, resolutions, failure, and SUCCESS. Most people want to become something or doing something for themselves, belonging to families or friends. That's why create an idea, a way to survive, to make money, or to feel good, and it is crucial for everyone.

Becoming an entrepreneur, not something easy, but having the right mindset will help you make that journey pleasant daily. That will help you set SMART goals and able to accomplish them.

The one who never tries that's the loser because failure is another form of getting somewhere. Don't be frightened to start your own business because what people will call failure could be the experience you need to concretize your dreams.

TABLE OF CONTENT

Contents

INTRODUCTION

The human desire is to treat their loved ones like a king and buy everything their loved ones will like. However, It is not always accessible to discover a way to do so. Because by staying as an employee, your freedom conditioned, and the money you made will also package. That more likely to become very difficult to accomplish.

There is a way, and you can be the chief of your destiny, of your time, and your freedoms. That's the way of the entrepreneurial. However, as an entrepreneur, if you want to be successful, you need to build a strong base. As solid construction must have strong support, a successful entrepreneur must have a strong core.

This book will help you resolve this problem by showing you exactly what you need to be a successful entrepreneur. You will learn in this book: what kind of company will fit your budget, what type of business you are good at, how to develop a team, how to evaluate your action, activities, expenses as you go. What kind of finance will best fit your type of company? Why customer service is essential for a company to survive> Learn how to create a communication plan. How to minimize your weakness and use your strength and how to lead and manage.

Great reading and enjoy.

Chapter I

Components of a company

A company or an organization is composed of many parts. For the organization to be operative, each component must be in good working order. Each piece must fit and work conjointly with other sections to reach the perform optimally. To do so, you will have to improve communication, productivity, effectiveness; and achieve strategic goals. To get organizational efficiency, you will need to have a plan with:

1. Customer Service and Performance Results, serving customers, and producing a quality product occupies central importance. Without this target, the organization is aimless—performance results from direct attention to individual and corporate productivity and efficiency. Employees are routinely informed about the organization's progress toward

established goals and objectives. You will be able to learn more about customer service later in chapter V.

2. Leadership, one such paradigm challenge, involves the distinction between leadership and management. One expert expresses it this way, "Managers are people who do things right, while leaders are people who do the right thing." – Warren Bennis, "On Becoming a Leader. "There is no debate that influential leaders can make a substantial difference in an organization's ability to thrive in an environment of persistent change. Contemporary thinking on the subject describes leadership as determining an organizational direction and then influence other people to follow that direction. What can make a person a great leader or a great manager? Details in chapter VIII.

3. Strategic Planning, a clear strategic plan, is crucial because it helps align the efforts of departments and individuals. It establishes priorities and determines how the organization's resources allocated. A strategic plan defines goals and objectives that will assist management in assessing progress toward the desired future state described in the vision.

4. Structure, an environment where everyone knows what needs to accomplish. Why it needs to achieve it, and to what standard. Accept complete responsibility for your staff. You choose the right people, you assign them, and you manage them with the expectation of excellence.

5. Human Resources Development and Management, the organization builds and maintains an environment that encourages performance

excellence, full participation, meaningful work, and personal and organizational growth.

6. Process Management, Process management areas that might consider for improvement include such things as:

1. Product or Service Development Processes: Those processes that are directly related to creating products and services.

2. Service Delivery Processes: Those processes involved delivering products and services to customers and stakeholders.

3. Marketing Processes are those processes that are involved in marketing products or services to customers and stakeholders.

7. Information and Data Analysis, an organization that seeks to be real and to meets the needs of its customers in a rapidly changing environment, must rely on accurate data to monitor customer satisfaction and to measure progress toward goals and objectives outlined by the strategic plan.

You can never have organizational effectiveness if you do not have the right strategies at the right time. That's why I will show you the most useful strategic management, which will help you succeed. The strategic management process best implemented when everyone within the business comprehends the approach. The five stages of the development are goal-setting, analysis, strategy formation, strategy implementation, and strategy monitoring. You will never be talented enough to get to the success you expect if you do not master these concepts:

• Clarify Your Vision, recognizing these important facets: Primary, define both short- and long-term objectives. Also, identify the process of how to accomplish your goal. Lastly, adapt the progression for your staff, give each individual a task with which he can prosper. Keep in mind during this development, your goals to be detailed, realistic, and match the values of your vision.

• Gather and analyze information. In this phase, wrinkle as much information and data pertinent to accomplishing your dream. The scrutiny should be on thoughtful the needs of the business as a maintainable entity, its strategic direction, and identifying initiatives that will help your business grow. Scrutinize any external or internal matters that can affect your goals and objectives.

• Formulate a strategy, determine what resources the business currently has that can help reach the defined goals and objectives. Identify any areas in which the industry must seek external support. Their importance to your success should prioritize the issues facing the company. Once prioritized, begin formulating the strategy.

• Implement Your Strategy, and this is the achievement stage of the strategic supervision process. If the global strategy does not work with the business's current structure, a new system should install at the launch of this stage. Everyone inside the organization must be made clear of their tasks and duties. And how that fits in with the overall goal. For example, when no one knows is the duty they have, that is not healthy for a company.

And each step of your project put together ideas, build the training program, implement the empower program, employee support program, or others, you will always need to use the SMART technic to keep your goals on the right track. What is the SMART method means?

SMART

It is a method that will help you keep your vision close to the people; help stay realistic as you progress in your project. It is imperative to test everything you want or needs to do with that SMART method:

Explicitly, you define your goals with simple words that should make them vibrant and detailed. Otherwise, you won't be bright enough to focus your efforts or feel genuinely inspired to achieve it. There are these questions to ask yourself when you build your goals:

- What do I want to accomplish?
- Why is this goal important?
- Who is involved?
- Where is it located?
- Which resources or limits are involved?

Example

Imagine that you currently have two stores open, and you would like to open more stores. A precise goal could be; I want to gain the customer's positives reviews. To become known for my excellent customer service and my company's value, such as customers first, so I can build my reputation and be able to open more stores.

Measurable, having measurable goals, it's vital to track your progress and stay motivated. That will help you track the progress and remain fixated, meet your deadlines, and feel the enthusiasm of getting closer to accomplishing your goal.

For any measurable goal, you should address questions such as:

- How much?
- How many?
- How will I know when it accomplished?

Example
You might measure your goal of obtaining the resources you need to open a new store. By training qualified employees able to carry the company's philosophy and the skills to keep providing the quality of services in two years, I will open a quality store that can offer the same service.

Achievable, to be successful, your goals need to be attainable. They should stretch your abilities and remain possible. By setting up a reachable goal, you may be able to recognize previously overlooked opportunities or resources that can bring you nearer to it.

Try to answer these questions when setting up achievable goals:

- How can I accomplish this goal?
- How realistic is the goal?
- How can I overcome my constraints, such as financial factors?

Example

You might need to ask yourself whether financing required to open the new store is realistic, based on your current financial situation. You can ask yourself a question like: do you have enough trained personal? Are the necessary resources available to you? Can you afford to do it?

Relevant, you have to make sure your goals are matter to you and aligns with pertinent other destinations to your company in this step. You have to remember to involve anyone toward your goals, but you will still responsible for achieving it as the CEO of your company.

For any relevant goal, you must be able to answer YES to any of these questions:

- Does this seem worthwhile?
- Is this the right time?
- Does this match our other needs?

- Am I the correct person to reach this goal?
- Is it applicable in the modern socio-economic environment?

Example

You might want to gain money to open the new store within your company. Then is it the right time to undertake the necessary personal training, position of the new store, right marketing strategies, acquisition of equipment, and security of your new business?

Time, any goal, need a deadline, a target date to focus on it. That will help you choose your daily activities toward your goal precisely.

When sept up a time goal, you need to answer these questions:

- When?
- What can I do three months from now?
- What can I do two weeks from now?
- What can I do today?

Example

Gaining the finances you need might require additional loans or training for your new team. It's time to ask these questions: How long will it take you to acquire these funds? Do you need further training for your new team? It's imperative to give yourself a realistic time frame for completing the smaller goals that are necessary to achieving your final objective. After getting the right ideas about the components of a

THE BEST WAY TO BECOME SUCCESSFUL

company and the criteria you must use to keep everything you do close to the reality, it's time to define what type of business you want to start.

Chapter II

Type of business

Before talking about the stage of team development of your team, you need to determine what type of business you want your business to be? Base on the type of business you prefer, you will be more comfortable to develop your team strategy development. Opening a new business is very challenging, making exigent a lot of effort and sacrifices. But first, you need to recognize what type of business will more profitable for you. There are several models of place in the market like:

- Sole Proprietorship the Sole Proprietorship is the purest business form under which one can function a business. A single Proprietorship is not a legal entity. It merely refers to a person who owns the company and is personally responsible for its debts.

- A limited Liability Partnership is a partnership in which some or all partners have limited liabilities. It, therefore, can exhibit elements of businesses and corporations. Each partner is not accountable or liable for another partner's misconduct or negligence in an LLP.
- A limited Liability Company (LLC) is a corporate construction in the United States whereby the proprietors are not personally accountable for the business's debts or accountabilities. Limited liability companies are hybrid entities that combine the characteristics of a corporation with those of a partnership or sole Proprietorship.
- S corporation, An S corporation, for United States federal income tax, is a closely held corporation that makes a valid election to taxed under Subchapter S of Chapter 1 of the Internal Revenue Code. In general, wage any income taxes for S corporations.
- C corporation, below United States federal income tax law, refers to any corporation taxed distinctly from its owners. A-C corporation distinguished from an S corporation, which generally is not taxed separately.

Based on this information about the most types of companies, it will be much easier for you to pick one of them. It will be more efficient and profitable for you to create the right strategy; to attract people to your company. Most of all, keep the customers happy because the key to stay a long time in the business it's providing the right service where everyone feels welcome and essential.

After choosing your company type, you will need to make sure you have the right people to take care of the customers. When you want something perfect, the best way to get there is by putting effort through it. That's why it will be imperative to train, educate, and develop the right strategy to build your right team and help become the right fit for the job, that's call team development. How?

Five stages of team development

There are several ways to implement the right strategy for the development of your team. For a small business, let's start with these 5 (cinq) stapes:

- Forming in this stage, most squad members are cheerful and well-mannered. Some are concerned, as they haven't fully understood what kind of work the team will do. Others are merely excited about the task ahead. And as a leader, you play a dominant role at this stage, such as help them understand their role and be open; that way, they will feel comfortable asking questions.
- Storming often begins where there is a conflict between team members. Folks may work in different ways for all sorts of reasons, but if divergent working styles cause unexpected problems, they may

become frustrated. For example, team associates may contest your authority or jockey for position as their roles elucidated. Or, if you haven't defined evidently how the team will work, individuals might feel overwhelmed by their assignment, or they could be uncomfortable with the approach you're using.

- Norming is when people start to resolve their differences, appreciate colleagues' strengths, and respect your authority as a leader.
- The team reaches the performing phase, when hard work leads, without roughness, to accomplish the team's goal. The structures and progressions that you have set up sustenance this healthy.
- Adjourning, Team members who like routine, or who have developed close working relationships with colleagues, may find this stage difficult, mainly if their future now looks uncertain. For example, because of a remodel, some of them have to work a different schedule. Or A project teams exist for only a fixed period, and even permanent groups may disband through organizational restructuring. As a leader, be flexible.

The most significant way to lead is; by example, and the leader must be particular when asking someone to do something. It will be more efficient if everyone knows what is next after each activity. One way to make that happen it's by taking all these five staples of team development and make them work like one step.

Because of the lack of one step of team development in your administration, your team development could be challenging and raise countless conflicts. For example, Chris tells Jacques a way to do things, and Andrew shows Jacques a different way and asks him to do it that way that can cause conflict. To go a little further, I know in my workplace a significant variance between two managers just because of a lack of principles, and either one wants to build a display their way because the company did not predetermine the way the screen should make.

That's why it is crucial to put all the stages in one. And give a clear direction to everyone in a consistent manner. If not, you will take them one by one like that situation will consider as the conflict that's mean the storming stage because everyone tries to make things on their own. But this stage is critical because it is where countless employees fail. They start questioning the worth of what they do. For example, I have a team leader in my store. He always asks people to do the work he is supposed to do and talk about teamwork; one day, one of the employees refuses to do something for him because he feels overwhelmed by the workload. And that was the basis of a significant conflict between them.

Team success is weighty, and most people think the only way to have success is when you have everything plan, and everyone knows what they should do from A to Z daily. It's crucial to have a great structure to have success and stay around for long. Because when your work organized, you look more professional, and people give you more respect. To be sure you have the right financial plan in place for the type of business you choose, you need to determine what type of economic structure will be most profitable for your business?

Chapter III

Debt and Equity

Talking about becoming an entrepreneur, whether in the retail industry or another field, it is fascinating that help you improve yourself and help you decide on your future. But to accomplish that goal, usually, it is two ways to getting through funding a business; unless we are enough personal funds to start. There are debt or equity.

The debt market is the market someplace debt instruments traded. Debt devices are assets that require a fixed payment to the holder, usually with interest. Examples of debt instruments include bonds and mortgages.

The equity market is the marketplace for trading equity tools. Stocks are securities that are an entitlement on the earnings and assets of a corporation. A specimen of an equity instrument would be mutual stock shares, such as those traded on the New York Stock Exchange.

These two ways to get funds to start your small nosiness have their advantages and their disadvantages. Let's see what might be the most profitable for your company.

Debt financing: advantages and disadvantages

Debt Financing is borrowing money to finance the operations, and the growth of a company can be the right decision under the proper conditions. You will be in control of your business, but too much debt can inhibit the growth of the company. It does have its advantages and also its disadvantages:

Benefits of Debt:

- Control: Taking out a loan is temporary. The relationship ends when the debt repaid. The lender does not consume any say in how you run your business.
- Taxes: Loan interest is tax-deductible, whereas dividends paid to shareholders are not.
- Predictability: Principal and interest payments stated in advance, so it is easier to work these into your business's cash flow. Credits could be short, medium, or long term.

Disadvantages of Debt:

- Qualification: You must have acceptable credit ratings to qualify.

- Fixed payments: Principal and interest payments must make on specified times without fail. Businesses that have random cash flows might have complications making loan payments. Declines in sales can create severe problems in meeting loan payment dates.
- Cash flow: Taking on too much debt makes the business more likely to have problems meeting loan costs if cash flow declines. Investors will also see the industry as a higher risk and be reluctant to make additional equity investments.
- Collateral: Lenders will typically demand those individual assets of the company held as collateral, and you will be obligatory to guarantee the loan personally.

Equity financing: Advantages and disadvantages

With equity money from investors, you are relieved of the pressure to meet the deadlines of fixed loan payments. However, you have to give up some control of your business. And often have to consult with the investors when making significant decisions. You are no longer the company; you have to share all the sensitive information to the investor. Does it a good fit for a new entrepreneur?
Benefits of Equity:
- Less risk: You have less chance with equity financing because you don't have any fixed monthly loan payments to make. That can be incredibly helpful with startup businesses that may not have positive cash flows during the early months.

18

- Credit complications: If you have credit problems, equity financing might be the only choice for funds to finance growth. Even if debt financing offered, the interest rate may be too high, and the payments too steep to be tolerable.
- Cash flow: Equity bankrolling does not take funds out of business. Debt loan reimbursements take funds out of the company's cash flow, reducing the money wanted to finance growth.
- Long-term arrangement: Equity investors do not expect to accept an immediate coming back on their assets. They have a long-standing interpretation and also face the opportunity of losing their money if the business fails.

Weaknesses of Equity:

- Cost: Equity investors expect to obtain a return on their money. You, business owner, must be willing to share some of the company's profit with your equity partners. The amount of money rewarded to the partners could be higher than the interest rates on debt financing.
- Loss of Control: You will have to give up some control of your company when you take on supplementary investors. Equity partners want to have a power of speech in making the decisions of the business, especially the big decisions.
- Potential for Conflict: All the partners will not always agree when making decisions. These conflicts can erupt from different visions

for the company and disagreements on management styles. You must be willing to deal with these differences of opinions.

We recommend you as a new entrepreneur to raise funds through equity because that will help you stay debt-free. And as a new entrepreneur, you will need advice from different people who could be your investors. If you have a strong strategy plan base on the value of your company, you will be able to communicate with all your investors and find common ground.

Equity financing is an excellent fit for you. Instead of raising money through debt financing is a time-bound action where the borrower needs to reimburse the loan and interest at the end of the agreed period. Equity financing will give you peace of mind and deserve all these new communities with the same charism.

Equity financing will allow your company to acquire funds without incurring commitment. On the other hand, delivering a bond does grow the debt burden of the bond issuer because contractual interest payments must pay; unlike dividends, they cannot be reduced or suspended.

After determining the right financial investment for your company, you need to be sure you have the right strategy in place for the type of business you choose in chapter II. Do you need to determine what kind of leader you want for your business?

THE BEST WAY TO BECOME SUCCESSFUL

Chapter IV

Leadership

There are several ways to lead, but everyone has a way to seem like the right one to do it. In the past, I used to train people and the approach to do it for me was participative or democratic. I love when people share their opinion and open to hearing new things from others. Among all the types of leadership, I will explain the different styles of leadership, the relationship between power and leadership, the organizational requirements for exceptional leadership, and the importance of organizational success.

There are many styles of leadership, and I recommend these five most styles of leader whom almost everyone agrees they are noteworthy and mostly use:

- The visionary leader is an entrepreneur and a big thinker and may be considered a revolutionist or a dreamer. Example: The CEO of Amazon, with a single idea, changes the way many people thinking about shopping. And The x and Y built a fun place for people to come to drink Kraft beer and be with their friends have fun.

- The transformational leader seeks to motivate workers by inspiring them to work hard for a loftier goal. Example: Alphabet Inc. CEO Larry Page, who is recognized for his inspiring work philosophy, "We should be structure things that don't exist." He is creative and joint while expecting his subordinates to bring their best-advanced ideas.

- The Pacesetter style has exceedingly high standards for performance and expects those who work for them to be just as preoccupied as they are about doing things faster and better.

- The Democratic Leader this style allows the leader to collectively wisdom the group. But a consensus-building tactic can be disastrous in times of crisis when momentous events demand quick decisions.

- The Affiliative Leader is the social glue of their organization. They focus on building secure connections between employees. They are team players, working to develop self-esteem and giving people a feeling of being "in it together. Example: A grocery store where every department communicates and shares the same office space to build a good relationship.

For a new business, the best style of leadership will be the democratic one. Because that will help everyone participle and what others bring to the table could improve the management team creates the best training program and smart strategies for the proper well of the company. Does it exist a relationship between power and leadership?

The concepts of power and leadership have much in common. Passion is the exercise of leadership, and direction is only well-defined if you have the ability. Honestly, it is unthinkable that a leader should not have control. Consequently, the exercise of impact is a central part of most of the definitions of leadership. However, power is not equivalent to an effect on another person's behavior. But that does not mean the direction and authority are the same things. Power indicates coercion, influence, command, and in any organization, these have to activate to accomplish specific tasks, but the "leadership act represents a choice of these instruments. The principal function of a leader is to persuade, influence, motivate and inspire. In my book, I describe most of the characteristics of a great leader.

Motivation is the most coaching. It is imperative because, without that, you can't talk about business. I have a particular reason to make motivation as the biggest one. I want everyone in my company to be able at the end of the day to feel great for what they did throughout the day. Every single time they come back, I want them to have the same feeling.

A healthy business starts with a team very motivated to make other people happy or feel welcome. If the employees are not motivated, the customers will not come a second time because they will not find that enthusiasm. They are waiting to feel welcome and appreciated by the entrance. But it is difficult you find the right way to motivate employees.

THE BEST WAY TO BECOME SUCCESSFUL

According to some studies, the motivation of employees depends on what kind of leader you are. As a new small business owner, you will find people who have the characteristics of a real leader. What are the indicators of a great leader?

- Motivation, when the leader shows a personal commitment to hard work and innovative approaches to problem-solving, employees typically value these things too. Leaders deliver incentives to employees, such as bonuses and other financial rewards, to increase production.

- Team Building, leaders need to take extra steps to ensure that the virtual team communicates clearly. For example, they are using all the features of web-based conferencing software and webcams, such as surveys and polls. The leader can conduct physical and virtual meetings that enhance interaction. That's leading to organizational effectiveness.

- Change, the leader minimizes distractions for his employees and helps them manage transitions to new working conditions. For example, when your company installs a new software package to handle accounting transactions, the leader guarantees that all employees who will use the system get the training they need in advance of the implementation.

- Mentoring, the leader provides workshops in demonstration skills, negotiation, business penetration, project management, and other leadership capabilities. When the time comes, these subordinates can take over for departing leaders. Leaders contribute to long-term organizational effectiveness through succession planning, helping employees maintain a healthy work and life balance, and exemplifying high standards of ethical behavior.

Chapter V

Communication Plan

Human, by nature, always wants to experiment with their ideas to other people and want to make other people do things differently. To prime their plans, the human need to have to know whom their concept will expose. Those ideas will not be able to get to others if they don't have a channel. That's why it is essential when we have a message, we know to who communicate, we need a frequency to execute the project. It's a simple thing for a company to demonstrate the right way with its customers; the company needs to have a great message, great messengers, and choose the right channel.

The company you want to create must conquer customer loyalty. To do so, you will introduce a better communication plan base on customer's values, followed by the evaluation plan. Which will help you stay on track? Before then, what should be the purpose of your communication plan?

A communication plan is a policy-driven approach to providing employees and customers with information. The program should also address who has the authority to communicate confidential or sensitive information and how data disseminated. Finally, the plan should define what communication channels employees and managers will use to solicit feedback from customers and how communication is documented and archived.

Your communication plan should accomplish many things like:

- Training on technic of interaction with customers for all the employees
- Define my key audiences
- Create messages base on customers values
- Identify media channels
- Establish a timetable
- Evaluate the results

If into the communication plan, you don't have a clear idea about what your audience is, it will be challenging to build a message and be able to communicate with the right channels. The communication plan is crucial, and its purpose must be clear and precise.

You need to explain how you will evaluate the success of your plan. What will you measure to ensure that you are making improvements in customer communication?

To become better than others, you have to go back and reconsidered the progress you have made on each step of your communication plan. It is also true for any company. The best way to be sure you are on the right track is by going back and look at the way you deal with customers. Most importantly, look at the way you evaluate the communication plan base on customer's values. You must implement a system able to help you:

- Get feedback every month from customers.
- Get feedback every two weeks from employees to give them more knowledge via training.
- Observe the way they communicate with the customer on the phone or face to face.
- Observe the non-verbal of the employee when interacting with a customer.

Clarity makes things simple. To ensure customers will understand who you are, what you do, and how you can help them. The training of necessary communication skills for your employees it the best way to help the employees been professional and able to provide a great job. You cannot give what you don't have. Before asking them to deliver better than themselves, providing the right training is very important. With the proper training and the right communication plan, your company will be better on the field. To implement all these steps, you will need a strong customer service department in your company. How could you build that strong customer service department?

Chapter VI

Customer service

E every company needs to have an excellent customer service system. Because the success of a company depends on how the company interaction with customers. Anyone by entering a store or any business wants to have a good time meaning a pleasant experience. To make their experience enjoyable, your company has to provide excellent customer service. That's why before talking about customer experience, we will define what it is customer service and how providing excellent customer service affects the customer experience. How can you describe customer experience?

Customer experience is your customers' holistic perception of their experience with your business or brand. That could be by navigating on your website, entering in person into your business. Everything you do can impact your customers' perception and their decision to keep coming back or not. It is so imperative to give your customers a great impression from start to finish. Excellent customer experience is the key to success. The better experience customers have, the more repeat customers and constructive reviews you'll receive, while simultaneously reducing the friction of customer complaints and returns.

On top of these things, customer feedback is very informative. You gather information from your customers about their experience with your product, service, website, or business as an entire. You can use this comment to improve customer experience by removing or reducing areas of friction and increasing positive touchpoints. What is customer service?

Customer service is everything you do when you interact with a customer from salutation to see you next time. That's means by greeting the customer, and you have the responsibility to show the customers their presence is very important for you and appreciate. You have to make yourself available to help the customers find whatever they might need. You have created a desirable situation for the customers and feel comfortable to talk to you to ask questions or make complaints. Without customer service, no one to do those things, and without these actions, no business. That's why customer service is the heart of a business. Without excellent customer service, any business cannot stay long around.

To have excellent customer service, you need great leaders and great managers. As described in chapter IV, a great leader is the one who leads by example, which shows the team how to do things and empower them to take the initiative to create an excellent experience for customers. On the other hand, a great manager is the one who can follow-up, and mostly the one who controls, evaluates and sets up goals for the company. The leading reason customer service is essential is that that department in any company can create an atmosphere of organizational success.

Proper management provides services to the community in an appropriate, efficient, equitable, and sustainable manner. That can only achieve if critical resources for service provision, including human resources, are valuable. For that, your company will need all the requirements to help the leader to be what he should be; a person who persuade, to influence, to motivate, and to inspire. The organizational condition is what will help the company to build a real structure able to help the employee's growth and satisfy the customers. How important is that?

Success is a commitment to management practices that treat people as assets. That's why a company needs to have excellent organizational leadership that will lead it to stretch to success. In the case of your company, as a new entrepreneur, for a better result, you need to put in place a formal structure able to help the leader lead the company to success for a long time. Because with good organizational success, every employee will know what they expect from and work to achieve that goal, and when everyone reaches their destination, the company makes his goal also. Organizational success is significant for any company.

Chapter VII

Strength and weaknesses

Any company which wants to be successful need to have a system well done and work correctly for the good of customers. That's why their customer service needs to be effective. To ensure the effectiveness of your company, you must know your Customer service strengths and weaknesses. What could consider as strengths or weaknesses to a customer service department?

Strengths:
- The strength of a company starts with the value of their philosophy. Everything you do that should be philosophy related. Any action, policy, training program should value the basics of the company that is the company philosophy.
- A strength company, their philosophy always base on customers' value, care of the

feelings of each customer, and trait them with the same respect.

- Technology and social media can be an excellent opportunity for you to provide excellent customer service and establish your legacy in the field. Offering the same quality of service online will give you perfect visibility, which could help your business grow.

- How your company's customer service provides a distinct advantage over the competition should look like it? Your customer service is different because of that based on customer value and respect. The philosophy of pleasing customers has to establish at the beginning of your foundation. And keep that as long your company exists. That should see as the identity of your company.

- How does your company exceed its customers' expectations? The minute you walk into one of your stores, there is a guy outside who greets you with a 'Hello, sir. How do you do?' They go a step ahead, make you feel comfortable, and appreciate it.

Weaknesses:
- The way you digitalize your system might be a weakness.
- The lack of formation or follow up could be seeing as a weakness.
- Unavailable products or delays on customers' orders might be considered a weakness.

THE BEST WAY TO BECOME SUCCESSFUL

All these potential weaknesses could improved. We believe if your management team works together, you can define it away with a great strategy to reduce the risk related to those weaknesses. That way, everyone will keep trying their best to go the extra mile to help customers and make their shopping experience a pleasure. As every athlete before any competition, reevaluate their chance to win; you will have to do the same before starting your company. What is the best way to review your goals?

Chapter VIII

SWOT Analysis

E verything in life has two big faces. Strength and weakness. For someone to know how to use his advantage in his favor and reduce the impact of his vulnerability. This person must be getting to know them. As a new entrepreneur, the same things apply to your company. To avoid your weaknesses and use your strength well, the SWOT is crucial for your company. What SWOT means:

Strengths

- Employees' attitudes make sure your employees treat customers with a lot of respect and knowledge.

- Leadership in product innovation, be sure all your employees and your system are amicable for customers to use.

- Excellent customer service; be sure customers' value at your company; it is the main reason you open your doors.

36

- High integrity, make sure every employee does things right, and avoid lying.

Weaknesses

- The product, by lack of information out of work and customers, disappointed, could be one.
- Shelves some of the shelving need replacement or cleaning.
- Sign, the open and off character does not show visible.
- The price for some products, the prices are too high.

Opportunities

- Market Development, you can use your website to expand your market target.
- Product Development, you can personalize featuring or new products to change the flavor or increase customers' value.
- Diversification, you can try or adopt a new featuring or a new design for some product already in the store.

Threats

- Price Competition, the other companies have the same products, but you use a coupon to lower the price.
- New Products of the competitors, lance a new line of products at a low price.
- New Competitors, some new companies, open their doors and lance a sale promotion.
- Running a Free Device Promotion, some companies attract people to come inside of their business.

All the elements in the SWOT Analysis because it's All-In-One. I cannot talk to one without the others, and they are all related.

Your company has to pay great attention to customers' value because; one reason which will keep your company stays, in the long run, it's customers' value. That's why the service after purchase is significant. I choose the service after purchase as the big proposition of value because customers love having an easy way to return or exchange their products recently bought.

SWOT analysis is very important for any business, even more for new business. Because that will help you adjust or rebuild specific strategies to conquer more customers and stay in place for long. Never take anything for granted, always analyses your action, and always try to reduce your weaknesses to capitalize more on your strengths.

ACKNOWLEDGMENT

First and foremost, praises and thanks to God, the Almighty, for His showers of blessings.   Throughout   my thoughtfulness to complete the book successfully.

I am incredibly grateful for what life has offered me. My heartfelt thanks to my wife and my family. For their acceptance and patience during the process, I am spending much time away from them.

I am amazingly grateful to my parents for their love, prayers, caring, and sacrifices for my educating and formulating my upcoming.

I am very much gratified, to my wife

and my two daughters for their love, understanding, prayers, and continuing support to complete this book.

Also, I express my thanks to my brothers, sisters, and sister in law for their support and valuable prayers. A Special thanks go to my elder brother Barthelemy J. Demezier for the keen interest shown to complete this book.

I thank the Tuition Reimbursement Program of the management of Publix Super Markets for their support of my Business Management College degree.

In conclusion, my thanks go to all the people, Facebook friends, Instagram friends, what's up friends who have supported me to complete the book directly or indirectly.

ABOUT THE AUTHOR

Francois Demezier is an excellent author who has trying, struggling, known failure, and success during his life. He wants to show with you the best way to transform your letdown into success. That's the reason for the existence of this book.

Mr. Demezier studied Philosophy, Theology, Sciences of Education, Ethics, Sales of Automobiles, Notary Public, Life Insurance, Annuities, and Business Management.

Mr. Demezier worked in Haiti as Trainer/Manager between 2006 to 2010, responsible for a program of training in techniques of advocacy for a body of Human Rights base in Canada. He is working at Publix Super Markets in general management since 2011 and helping people as a financial advisor and Life Insurance broker since 2017.

Mr. Francois Demezier wants to show you in this book that you should never give up and always find a purpose in your life no matter what you do. Success is not just a word. Success will be your results when you have faith and confidence in what you do. Always do your best and try to help others, and the rest in God's hands.